23925

MUFFIN

MUFFIN

Judith Gwyn Brown

74-61

Abelard-Schuman New York · London

Library of Congress Catalogue Card Number: 72-1541
ISBN: 0 200 71895 9 Trade
ISBN: 0 200 71896 7 GB

Published on the same day in Canada by Longman Canada Limited.

NEW YORK	LONDON
Abelard-Schuman	Abelard-Schuman
Limited	Limited
257 Park Avenue So.	158 Buckingham Palace Road SW1
10010	and
	24 Market Square Aylesbury

An Intext Publisher

Printed in the United States of America

For the staff of the Picture Collection,
New York Public Library

Muffin was a shaggy puppy born in a box filled with shreds of cut paper. She lived with her mother and brothers and sisters in the country store of Mr. Prop.

When boys and girls came into the shop, pointing and laughing and choosing the puppy they liked best, Muffin dug under the shredded papers. She put her head between her paws and hid where it was warm and dark. No one wanted a shy puppy and no one chose Muff.

One by one, Muffin's brothers and sisters were taken to new homes, and at last her mother was put out to guard the gate. Muffin was the only puppy left in the store, and Mr. Prop marked down her price.

A week later, a car drove into the yard. Maggie ran up the steps and burst through the door. Today was Maggie's birthday and her father had promised her a dog, a puppy to share her room at last. Maggie knew she would love the first dog she saw.

She grabbed Muffin out of the box and kissed her.
Swinging the puppy high above her head, she carried
her to the car.

Happiness filled Maggie's eyes and she did not see
that Muffin shrank away from her as they drove toward
the city. Maggie welcomed her home.

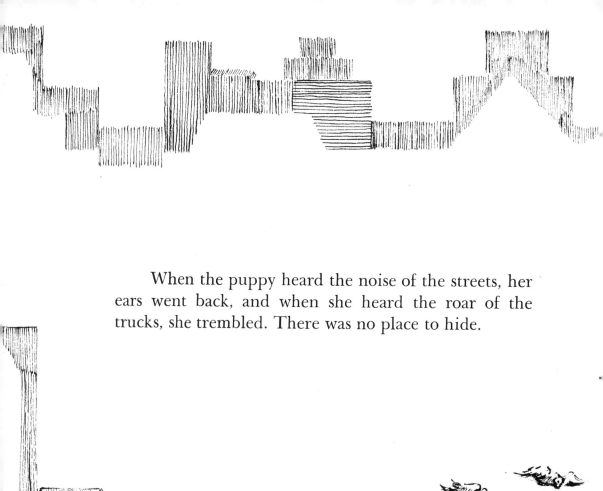

When the puppy heard the noise of the streets, her
ears went back, and when she heard the roar of the
trucks, she trembled. There was no place to hide.

Maggie carried Muffin into her room and set her down. Muffin looked up and peered all around. The chairs were high, and the bed with its patchwork quilt was tall above her. With wide eyes, Muff fled scampering under the chest of drawers where it was dark.

Maggie lay on the floor and whispered, "Muffin, please don't be afraid. I will take care of you and we will go to the park. And I will give you birthday parties, and tell you all my secrets." But Muffin only pushed back into the darkness and would not come out from beneath the chest.

In the evening, Maggie brought the best bit of her own dinner and stretched out her hand to Muff, but the puppy would not leave her hiding place.

That night under the chest of drawers, Muffin whimpered and cried for her dog mother and for her loneliness. Maggie got up in the dark and put her best rag doll beside the puppy to chew for comfort.

After school the next day, Maggie skipped to the park, tugging Muffin through the busy streets. The autumn leaves were crisp and the frightened puppy snuffled under them for something she remembered: a tongue to lick her face, a warm belly and padded paws. She listened in the crushed leaves for the yaps and grunts of other puppies, but there was nothing.

She pulled away from Maggie.
With an aching heart,
Maggie carried her home.

Soon the days grew cold with snow. When Maggie brought Muff back from the park, ice clung to the dog's shaggy coat. Maggie warmed the frozen paws with her own hands, but the puppy still drew away.

At last Maggie's mother said, "Maggie dear, Muffin is unhappy here. I think we had better send her back to the country."

Maggie's father said, "I've always wanted a larger dog anyway. Let's find another pup for you, a collie or a hunting hound."

Maggie shook her head and tried with all her might
to make Muff like her. She combed her own hair over
her face to look like Muff and peered through the
tangles into the puppy's eyes. She even tried to learn
to bark. But Muffin sat silently all day under the chest
of drawers and would not come out to play.

One morning Maggie woke up with a sore throat. She went with her mother to the doctor who told her she must have her tonsils out. Then Maggie's mother took both of Maggie's hands in her own and spoke quietly as she did when something serious happened. "Tomorrow we must take you to the hospital where they will make you well, dear. Everything will be all right," she said. But Maggie could feel her heart beat inside her.

That night Maggie threw her arms around Muffin and held her tight. For the first time the puppy did not pull away.

In the morning, Maggie left with her mother and father to go to the hospital. As the car drove away, Muffin came out from under the chest of drawers. She sniffed Maggie's shoes and schoolbooks and her sweater which lay on a chair. In the afternoon, she listened for Maggie at the door, but Maggie was not there. After a while, the puppy heard steps in the hall, but they were not Maggie's steps. Muffin waited all day.

In the evening, Maggie's mother took Muffin for a walk. She walked quickly down the dark streets and did not stop to put her hand on Muff's head when a truck roared by.

When they returned to the house, Muffin's tail was down and she slunk away to her hiding place.

Maggie's father and mother talked.

"Poor Maggie. We must send that dog away. The animal was a big mistake."

"Let's wait until Maggie is well, and then call Mr. Prop and ask him to take the creature back."

The next day Maggie came home from the hospital. She was put to bed among her pillows with the patchwork quilt to her chin. Tired and alone, she stared at the chest of drawers and at the dark cave-place beneath it. Then she raised herself up on one elbow and tried to call Muff. But her throat was sore and only a squeaky croak came out.

Maggie tried again and again to call the puppy but she could not. She leaned back on her pillows, too sad to move.

The morning light grew yellow in the room.

Suddenly Maggie heard a small scraping sound. She leaned over the bed and watched as a black wet nose and furry head poked out from under the chest of drawers. Muffin stood in a patch of sunlight, blinking and peering up at her. Then, swiftly, the puppy turned and scampered back under the chest.

Soon from the dimness of the chest, Maggie saw a quivering nose sniffing once more. The puppy squeezed out from her hiding place and slowly took a step toward the bed. Then another. She gave one small wag of her tail and her shy paws stepped forward little by little.

Bending over, Maggie put out her arms and pulled the puppy up onto the bed.

Muff's tail was wagging wildly now, and tears ran down Maggie's cheeks as she stuffed the puppy under the covers. She dried her eyes on the soft ears as Muffin burrowed into her arms and licked her face.

Then all at once, to the puppy, the patchwork quilt was as good as shreds of paper, and Maggie was all of her sisters and brothers and mother too.

When spring came, Maggie and Muffin ran through the streets to the park. They rolled in the tangled grass together, and soon thistles and clover were clinging to Maggie's hair and to Muffin's soft, shaggy fur.